TEN
Confessions
FOR
LIVING

PRAYERS AND CONFESSION FOR LIVING A GOD CONSCIOUS LIFE

ILYA GOLDEN

Denise,
You are so special to me. Keep being a God conscious wife.

Love,
Pastor Sy

Ten Confessions for Living
Prayers and Confessions for Living a God Conscious Life

Copyright ©2016 Ilya Golden.
PRINTED IN THE USA
ISBN-13: 978-1532891175
All rights reserved. No part of this book maybe reproduced in any form, stored in a retrieval system, or transmitted in any form by any means- electronic, mechanical, photocopy, recording or otherwise, without the prior written permission of the publisher.

Scripture references: the New King James version. (1982). Nashville: Thomas nelson. Unless otherwise noted

Cover by VI LUXE Designs Branding Studio, Plano, Texas
Back cover author photo © Anthony Douglas Photography

Dedication

This book is dedicated to Pastor Bridget Hilliard who inspired me to write confessions and who so genuinely made me believe that the prayers I prayed, God would hear and respond.

Acknowledgement

To my mom, thank you for training to use my gifts to glorify God.

To my husband and my beautiful children. You guys make my life so colorful and beautiful. Thank you for always believing in me, making me smile and keeping me on my toes.

To my friends, who sharpen and make me better and Amazing Church family for your support and love. I pray that this book will in some way help you Restore Hope and Love People to Life!

To my friend Barbara Calloway, thank you for reading this over and over and for making sure that I met my deadline.

Ilya

Foreword

There are very few people in the world that I know that have the ability to watch the words that come from their lips with consistency. It is a difficult feat, but attainable. *Hebrews 11:3* says "...that the worlds were framed by the words of God..." this powerful principle is revealed and when coupled with *Proverbs 18:21* "...that life and death is in the power of the tongue." This should give you the clarity you need and the confidence you need to speak the world you want to live in and the life you want to have, by using the power of confession. Now confession without prayer and a surrendered heart to God is just a formula and void of a heart after God. We see this all the time, but not here, Ilya Golden has desired to be simply sincere, an approach to this subject that makes prayer and confession partners with a heart towards pleasing God. Take this book as a reference guide for your devotion and prayers in the time of need.

Derrick A. Golden
Lead Pastor, Amazing Church

Table of Contents

Dedication 5

Acknowledgement 6

Foreword 7

Introduction 11

Matters of the Heart 13

The Right Perspective 19

Your Thought Life 25

Fear is A Lie 31

Wisdom 37

My Worship 43

Gracefulness 45

Daughter of A Father 55

My Family 61

I Must Have Balance 67

Introduction

Whenever I've faced a health challenge I believe those were some of my most vulnerable times. Had I not known that the promise of God is for those of us that are considered His children, I'm not sure how I would have made it through those seasons. I've had some serious anxiety in my 40 plus years of living here, whether it was my own or someone else's health challenge. Fear or doubt has always attempted to do what it was created to do, that is, to try and cause me not trust the One who heals. My daughter dealt with a health challenge for years. She's a creative, gifted and an athletic young lady that I have loved from the moment I laid eyes on her. I remember the day that she said mom would you pray for me and of course I said yes! Not only did I pray for her, but I wrote several confessions for her to pray over herself. Currently she's enjoying life, pursuing a career and God answered our prayers.

Here's one of the Confessions written for my daughter:

It is God's will for me to be healed. It is Gods will for me to live a life of abundance. Lord restore my health and heal every wound {Jeremiah 30:17}. I pray for strength and wholeness to come to my body now. I know that you are for me and nothing is too hard for you. My family is in agreement with me for healing and your word says if two of you agree on earth concerning anything they ask it will be done { *Matthew 18:19*}. Remove the pain, inflammation and whatever the root cause of this affliction. I command you to leave and never come back again {*Nahum 1:9*}. I believe that my faith and the words that I speak is bringing healing to my body, in Jesus' name amen.

In this book you will find stories, prayers and confessions. Confessions are words that are spoken in agreement with the word of God. I believe these confessions will inspire you to live well, an amazing life promised to you in the word of God.

I have written and formatted this book in a way that you can tear pages out and frame them in your home, your job or business. By allowing your words to frame your world (I love frames), so frame them, because the more you see the words and confessions the more you will say them.

Enjoy and may the favor of God and His word come to pass in your life!

Matters of the Heart ♥

In my life there have been so many things that could have taken me to a place where I would not have been willing to trust, love or live. I remember the day that I got the revelation that God loves me. I'll tell you that later in this book. Just know that my heart was changed forever. I don't know what you are facing or what could have stolen your heart away from the ability to trust, love or live. But we see in *Psalm 51* that God knew we would need a passage that could bring us comfort and ensure that our spirit would be able to anchor our confession in times like these.

PSALM 51:10

Create in me a clean heart, O God,
And renew a steadfast spirit within me.

Prayer

God, as I live this life here in the world, help me to keep my heart clean and focused on you and your assignment for my life. In Jesus' name – Amen!

CONFESSION

Father I ask that you would create in me a clean heart and renew a right spirit within me. Cause a spirit of joy to arise within me. Today I seek you and when I seek you with my whole heart I will find you. I have a choice as to what I allow into my heart and I declare that I am thankful, I am laughing, I am jumping for joy and I am singing your song.

The Right Perspective

Today's world has a perspective that is different from the Kingdom of God. With so many views and standards, we need to have the right understanding or better stated, a right perspective. Your perspective is how you view or see things and the filter we use for how we see circumstances, situations and perceive those outcomes. In *Proverbs 3:5* it is clear that if you have the perspective of the world, you could miss the benefits of the Kingdom. I have decided that I will see things the way of the Kingdom.

Proverbs 3:5

*Trust in the L*ORD *with all your heart,*
And lean not on your own understanding;

Prayer

God I thank you for giving me the strength to focus and see things the way you see and desire me to see them. I trust that you will help me to learn your ways and show me how you want me to live in Jesus' name! Amen.

CONFESSION

God your word is a lamp unto my feet and a light to my path. I choose to follow in your ways and lean not on my own understanding. Therefore, Father I have a Kingdom perspective, with an expectancy that You will guide and order my steps. Father I trust that you will direct my path as I continue to see from your perspective.

Your thought Life

I don't know if you are like me, but so much goes on inside my head, thoughts about everything. Those thoughts have the potential to overwhelm and cause anxiety. I want you to know that *Philippians 4:8* tells us what we should meditate on and *2 Corinthians 10:3 – 5* liberates us by sharing that our thoughts are powerful and that we should bring those thoughts and anything else that tries to rise above what the Word says, should be taken captive.

Philippians 4:8

Finally, brethren, whatever things are true, whatever things are noble, whatever things are just, whatever things are pure, whatever things are lovely, whatever things are of good report, if there is any virtue and if there is anything praiseworthy—meditate on these things.

2 Corinthians 10:3 – 5

For though we walk in the flesh, we do not war according to the flesh. 4 For the weapons of our warfare are not carnal but mighty in God for pulling down strongholds, 5 casting down arguments and every high thing that exalts itself against the knowledge of God, bringing every thought into captivity to the obedience of Christ

Prayer

God of peace, please keep my mind fixed on you and the Kingdom and keep my thoughts from running away with my confidence in You and Your promises for me, in Jesus' name, Amen!

CONFESSION

God you are Lord over my life! Help me to surrender my thoughts to Your authority, those things that are true, honorable, right, pure and beautiful. I bring every thought captive today and claim the victory in every area of my life including my thoughts.

Fear is A Lie

Fear is a liar and a very good one. Now I'm not an advocate of extremism, so some fear is healthy, we will discuss that at a later time, let's just say, I don't like to drive next to eighteen-wheeler semis during the rain. This is a natural fear. But the kind of fear that lies to you and keeps you from going forward and fulfilling purpose you must defeat! The way you defeat fear is not by ignoring it, but with boldness that confronts the deep hidden reasons for your fear. As we see in *1 John 4:18*, we are to find our confidence in the love that God has for us. A perfect love that comforts and confronts all your fears to allow you the strength you need to fulfill your purpose for being on the planet.

1 John 4:18

There is no fear in love; but perfect love casts out fear, because fear involves torment. But he who fears has not been made perfect in love.

Prayer

God I ask that you continue to surround me with your perfect love that overcomes all fear so that I can fulfill your call and purpose for my life, in the name of Jesus, Amen!

CONFESSION

God you are my refuge! I will not be afraid of the terror by night, nor the arrow by day. You are my rock and my salvation. I thank you for the angels that have been assigned to me. I have confidence in your Word. Where your love is, fear has to go.

Wisdom

Wisdom is the principle thing, you can ask God and He will grant it to you liberally. However, if you don't know what wisdom is, then you won't know what to do with it when you ask. We believe that wisdom is the proper application of the knowledge you presently have and the ability to gain insight on a subjects not been previously known. So wisdom is not only needed but should be sought and treasured when it is found.

Proverbs 19:8

8 He who gets wisdom loves his own soul; He who keeps understanding will find good.

Prayer

God I ask that you give me wisdom so that I may manage what I already know and insight to the things unknown. Lead me in the best path for making wise decisions in my life, in Jesus' name!

CONFESSION

Father in the name of Jesus I thank you for your wisdom and the goodness in my life that it produces. continue to give me the wisdom that only comes from You so that I may prove your wisdom is good here in the earth.

My Worship

A worshipper is one who honors God and responds to him with thanksgiving. My worship is personal and yet public. I've learned that it's more than a song that we sing or a dance to. It has more to do with the actions that we display and how we live that says, thank you. My Worship is how I say thank you. Thank you for creating me and for all that you have done for me. I'm going to represent you well. I'm going to be a light for the world to see, I promise I won't hide. I'll live in a way that people will see the good things that You do and I'll praise You with a pure heart.

John 4:24

24 God is Spirit, and those who worship Him must worship in spirit and truth."

Prayer

Father I ask that you receive my worship, I earnestly desire to please you, so help me to be a vessel that lives a life poured out of pure heart, in Jesus' name, Amen!

CONFESSION

Lord God, I thank you for giving me the opportunity to worship in spirit and in truth, to honor you with the fruit of my lips that proclaim who you are to me.

Gracefulness

The beauty of a lady comes in many forms from the manner in which she speaks, to the way she moves, how she takes care of herself, her family and business, to the way she holds her hands. There are many transactions that take place throughout the days, months and years. How you handle those transactions is exampled in *Proverbs 31* when we talk about our favorite girl!

Proverbs 31:25 – 29

She opens her mouth with wisdom,
And on her tongue is the law of kindness.
27 She watches over the ways of her household,
And does not eat the bread of idleness.
28 Her children rise up and call her blessed;
Her husband also, and he praises her:
29 "Many daughters have done well,
But you excel them all."
30 Charm is deceitful and beauty is passing,
But a woman who fears the LORD, she shall be praised.

Prayer

God grant me the peace to stand strong to be who you have made me to be, uniquely and wonderfully have you made me, I thank you for this most precious time to commune and represent You and the Kingdom in Jesus' name, Amen!

CONFESSION

Father I thank you for giving me the ability to walk in a manner that represents you well and honors what you intended when you created me; strong, bold and graceful, with the ability to execute Your will in and for my life.

Daughter of A Father

I am a girl who has never seen her earthly father and was molested by a man that I called father. So, my view of who or what a father was, was flawed. I wasn't sure how to be a daughter of a father, until the day I received a revelation while listening to a song and hearing the voice of God speak to me. *Psalm 68* has real meaning to a daughter like me. That day was a defining moment in my belief of who God was despite my previous experience with fatherhood. I am a daughter of an amazing Father that loves me and I don't have to do anything to earn His love nor will I ever lose it!

Psalm 68:4 – 5

Sing to God, sing praises to His name;
Extol Him who rides on the clouds,
By His name YAH,
And rejoice before Him.
5 A father of the fatherless, a defender of widows, Is God in His holy habitation

Prayer

Father God I ask in the name of Jesus that you reveal to me that I am your daughter and that you will never leave me nor forsake me and that you have a plan for my life. Your love for me never fails.

CONFESSION

I thank you God that I am your daughter and your enduring love reaffirms me and gives me the confidence I need to walk out and complete the call You have on my life.

Family

I love my family! Our time spent together at family meetings, listening to music, dancing, singing together and sharing stories about our days creates a bond that is beautiful. God has put us all in a family, whether we like it or not, if you are breathing you came into this planet and you are a part of a family. He designed the family for us to have relationships that would build us, train us and bless us according *Acts 3:25*.

Acts 3:25

25 You are sons of the prophets, and of the covenant which God made with our fathers, saying to Abraham, 'And in your seed all the families of the earth shall be blessed.'

Prayer

Father you created the family dynamic and I ask that you help me to continue to be an asset to my family and build us up so that we can as a family be a blessing here in the earth in Jesus' name, Amen!

CONFESSION

Lord I thank you for my family. I choose to honor my parents and I am submitted in the union established for me and my spouse. My children are blessed and will fulfill the purpose on their lives and shall be delivered from the hand of the enemy. My family is blessed coming in and when we go, we live in the best and favor surrounds us like a shield and your hand of protection will be with us all the days of our lives.

I Must have Balance

There are times in life when everything seems to run together. When that happens, it affects what we do, how we respond, the decisions that we make and it makes it difficult to hear the voice of God. It is vital for our lives that we are balanced, resting, making healthy and wise choices. What you value determines how you live. Take a moment listen to the voice of God, plan and position yourself to live well.

Isaiah 56:2

2   Blessed is the man who does this,
And the son of man who lays hold on it;
Who keeps from defiling the Sabbath,
And keeps his hand from doing any evil."

Prayer

Father I ask that you grant me the courage to always keep a Sabbath to refresh my body and to honor You in Jesus', Amen!

CONFESSION

I receive now the healing and refreshing that comes from honoring the Sabbath day, a time set aside to refresh and regroup and as a result I am blessed and living life to the fullest!

Made in the USA
San Bernardino, CA
24 April 2016